MW00468855

Faith in Difficult Times

Preston Condra | Kelly Condra

Faith in Difficult Times
Preston Condra and Kelly Condra
Sufficient Word Publishing

Published by Sufficient Word Publishing, Springdale, AR
A division of Sufficient Word Ministries
Copyright ©2020 Preston Condra and Kelly Condra

Limit of Liability/Disclaimer of Warranty: While the publisher and author have used their best efforts in preparing this book, they make no representations or warranties with respect to the accuracy or completeness of the contents of this book and specifically disclaim any implied warranties of merchantability or fitness for a particular purpose. No warranty may be created or extended by sales representatives or written sales materials. The advice and strategies contained herein may not be suitable for your situation. You should consult with a professional where appropriate. Neither the publisher nor author shall be liable for any loss of profit or any other commercial damages, including but not limited to special, incidental, consequential, or other damages.

Cover and Interior design: Madison Lux, *upwork.com/fl/madisonlux*
Interior photography: Linda Richards, *lindarichardsphotography.com*

Library of Congress Cataloging-in-Publication Data
Library of Congress Control Number: 2020906034
Preston Condra and Kelly Condra

Faith In Difficult Times
ISBN: 978-1-946245-10-6
Library of Congress subject headings:
1. REL012120 RELIGION / Christian Life / Spiritual Growth
2. REL006220 RELIGION / Biblical Studies / New Testament
3. REL006700 RELIGION / Biblical Studies / Bible Study Guides

2020

ATTENTION CORPORATIONS, UNIVERSITIES, COLLEGES AND PROFESSIONAL ORGANIZATIONS: Quantity discounts are available on bulk purchases of this book for educational, gift purposes, or as premiums for increasing magazine subscriptions or renewals. Special books or book excerpts can also be created to fit specific needs. For information, please contact Sufficient Word Publishing, *publisher@sufficientwordpublishing.com*

Table of Contents

The Operation of Faith

For whatsoever is born of God overcometh the world: and this is the victory that overcometh the world, even our faith. (1 Jhn 5:4)

If the average American was asked, "Do you have faith?" he would probably say, "Yes." If he was asked, "What is the object of your faith?" he might reply, "What does that mean?" Words like love, hope, and thankfulness are not nebulous concepts directed at nothing. They must have an object; faith must also. We love someone, hope for something, and are thankful to someone for something. As Christians, our faith is also in someone and something: Firstly, it is in Jesus Christ and His work on the cross; secondly, it is in the promises of God to the church. In general, the Christian faith is in the truthfulness, trustworthiness, reliability, and sufficiency of God's word, which contains both the saving Gospel message and the promises which describe and enable Christian living. If either of these were lacking, the Bible would be of no greater use than the advice of a friend. This begs the question: Are Christians using it merely as a soothing devotional or a source of advice among other sources? The Bible is not a book of "good ideas to consider." It is the very breath of God. It explains who God is, how He operates and what He wants from man. It defines the changes in His dealings with mankind, such as the shift from law to grace. The letters to the church in particular amount to a technical manual for accessing the power of God's grace. The ability to recognize, learn, and use those things which God has provided is necessary every day, so that one might live according to God's will. In difficult times, the ability to "plug in" to the grace of God can be absolutely vital.

To use what God has given, a Christian must understand what faith really is, how it works, and how it looks in operation so that it can be recognized. Faith is not wishful thinking. It is not an emergency back-up when all else has failed. It is not mystical;

it is based in fact. Faith is a conviction of mind that God has chosen to be His delivery system for blessing humanity. Understanding faith is important because it accesses salvation from the penalty for sin. Beyond initial salvation, it offers deliverance from the power of sin, the deception of Satan, and the distraction of the world's life-wasting activities and agendas. The Christian who believes God's word is free. He is filled up to overflowing with divine enabling power so that he does not quench His work within. In a word, he is "spiritual."

The spiritual Christian sees the world from God's viewpoint. He has a proper perspective about the things that happen in life and is able to navigate its many obstacles. In his spiritual condition he emanates the character of God, displaying wisdom and grace in whatever he does. He recognizes the attacks upon his attitude, priorities, desires and motives, counteracting them by renewing his mind with the teachings of grace. He knows that God has provided him with all he needs; therefore, his faith in God's promises makes them actual in his experience: he believes God has given him courage and he is brave. He knows God is kind, so he can be kind also. He knows the Holy Spirit is his teacher, so he makes time to study and learn. He knows that God will even give him the "want-to" for those things that he naturally would not want to do. His faith in God's word is the equivalent of saying, "Yes," to God, so that he can operate as a partner with God, operating according to God's will and weathering the difficulties of life with supernatural ability.

The scripture contains numerous calls to the believer: to evangelize, to mature, to be hospitable, to give, to help, to encourage, to forgive, and many more. It is not unusual for one verse to contain several. It would be impossible for any person to even come close to achieving the dozens of directives, let alone to keep them consistently. What a discouragement it would be to even try! But there is blessed relief in knowing that they are actually a call to let God do these things in us. Because they are by faith, it is He who produces them. It is not up to the believer to try to figure out how to make all these things happen.

If he could, he would not have needed to be saved because he would be perfect like Jesus Christ. It is helpful to keep in mind that the Christian life is not a busy-work program. It is an internal operation with internal and external results. It is an outworking of the quality of life that exists in eternity, the life that the members of the Godhead share. This life of love and joy is what God desires for every Christian, right now and forever. Eternal life is a quality of life which results from knowing God through Jesus Christ and resting in what He accomplished.

> *And this is life eternal, that they might know thee the only true God, and Jesus Christ, whom thou hast sent.* (Jhn 17:3)

To access eternal life, prepare for difficult times, and do God's will every day, a Christian must operate by faith. To do so, there are things that he needs to know and understand. The Spirit-filled Christian:

- Understands what faith is and how it operates so that he can use it.

- Agrees with God's viewpoint as revealed in his written word, including holding a correct perspective regarding the fleeting and temporary things of this world.
- Knows the promises of God so that he can direct his faith accordingly.
- Recognizes the outworking of faith in himself so that he can redirect his thinking and return to faith if it is lost.
- Trusts God's sufficiency no matter the appearance of things in this life or his feelings about them.

The Christian who lives by faith is one who believes that God can produce His character within him while he mows the lawn, cleans the house, cares for the children, does his job, sits in traffic, gets accused and abused by the world, and suffers the tragedies that are a normal part of a fallen world. For a Christian, faith is the way of daily life. It accesses the power of God's grace so that the Christian is not shaken by the difficult times nor stalled by the mundane. We, the authors, pray that this short volume will bless its readers with a better understanding of the operation and benefit of daily faith, so that when the most difficult times of life occur, accessing God's power will not be one of the difficulties.

Chapter 1

From Faith to Faith

For therein is the righteousness of God
revealed from faith to faith: as it is written,
The just shall live by faith. (Ro 1:17)

Faith is the doorway to a relationship with God. It is also the mechanism for living according to His will. It differs from wishful thinking in that its object is not a desire but is a person or a promise. One can only believe God for things that He has promised to do. One cannot "believe God" if there is no promise because in that case there is nothing to believe. Human desire places no obligation on God. In fact, many of those things for which humanity wishes are contrary to His purpose.

One can also believe "in" God, meaning to believe who He is and what He has done. For example, the object of faith for initial salvation is in the person of

9

Jesus Christ and in His work on behalf of mankind. Saving faith can be exercised by an unregenerate sinner; he is able to understand that he sins, that a penalty will be imposed, and that a divine person was his substitute in suffering that penalty. That divine person, Jesus Christ, is God the Son, the second person of the Trinity, and the one and only Savior, who took upon Himself human flesh so that he could be a perfect, infinite, sinless sacrifice for the infinite sins of the world.

> *In the beginning was the Word, and the Word was with God, and the Word was God. ... And the Word was made flesh, and dwelt among us, (and we beheld his glory, the glory as of the only begotten of the Father,) full of grace and truth. ... And I saw, and bare record that this is the Son of God.* (Jhn 1:1, 14, 34)

> *For he hath made him* to be *sin for us, who knew no sin; that we might be made the righteousness of God in him.* (2 Cor 5:21)

Not by works of righteousness which we have done, but according to his mercy he saved us, by the washing of regeneration, and renewing of the Holy Ghost... (Titus 3:5)

And walk in love, as Christ also hath loved us, and hath given himself for us an offering and a sacrifice to God for a sweetsmelling savour. (Eph 5:2)

...but now once in the end of the world hath he appeared to put away sin by the sacrifice of himself. (Heb 9:26b)

The sacrifice of Jesus Christ was propitiatory, meaning it completely satisfied the debt that man owed God for sinning against Him. The sinner who responds to the conviction of the Holy Spirit places his faith in the person of Jesus Christ: he is convinced of who He is, trusts in what He did, and is thereby delivered from the penalty for sin.

And he is the propitiation for our sins: and not for ours only, but also for the sins of the whole world. (1 Jhn 2:2)

Herein is love, not that we loved God, but that he loved us, and sent his Son to be the propitiation for our sins. (1 Jhn 4:10)

And every priest standeth daily ministering and offering oftentimes the same sacrifices, which can never take away sins: But this man, after he had offered one sacrifice for sins for ever, sat down on the right hand of God; (Heb 10:11-12)

For therefore we both labour and suffer reproach, because we trust in the living God, who is the Saviour of all men, specially of those that believe. (1 Tim 4:10)

The one who believes in the death, burial, and resurrection of Jesus Christ for his sins is spiritually regenerated, also known as born again or born from above. God has given him spiritual life by coming to indwell his human spirit. He is now a child of God, no longer separated from God by trespasses and sins.

Whereas faith for initial salvation is in a person, faith for Christian living is in the promises of God to the church; God's righteousness is revealed from initial faith to living by faith. His righteousness is credited to the one who believes the Gospel of Christ, making him no longer guilty in the eyes of God. In living by faith, the Christian displays God's righteousness.

Only a person who is born again can exercise faith in God's promises; he must be spiritually alive in order to comprehend them and access them for use. They are spiritual in nature and are not available to the natural man. A natural man is one who remains in the condition in which he was born; he has not been born again.

> *For what man knoweth the things of a man,*
> *save the spirit of man which is in him? even*
> *so the things of God knoweth no man, but the*
> *Spirit of God. Now we have received, not the*
> *spirit of the world, but the spirit which is of*
> *God; that we might know the things that are*
> *freely given to us of God. ... But the natural*
> *man receiveth not the things of the Spirit of*
> *God: for they are foolishness unto him: neither*
> *can he know* them, *because they are spiritually*
> *discerned.* (1 Cor 2:11-12, 14)

Faith in the promises of God to the church is to be used for daily living by the saints. Learning to walk by faith is something that a Christian continues to learn all of his life. When life's routine is interrupted by difficulties and hardship, one's faith often comes to the forefront: Its importance becomes more obvious as does its lacking. A time of trouble can be viewed by a Christian as a blessed opportunity to draw nearer to God in practice as he already is in his position in the body of Christ. He can abandon his double-mindedness and cling to God alone, trusting

Him to provide all that is needed throughout the time of trial. When those things in which one was trusting begin to slip away, whether job security, money, health, or people, the promises of God stand sure.

> *Draw nigh to God, and he will draw nigh to you. Cleanse your hands, ye sinners; and purify your hearts, ye double minded.* (Jas 4:8)

> *And ye are Christ's; and Christ is God's.* (1 Cor 3:23)

Chapter 2

The Mindset of Faith

Looking for that blessed hope, and the glorious appearing of the great God and our Saviour Jesus Christ; (Titus 2:13)

In order to access and utilize the promises of God, one must both believe in Him and believe Him. To believe in the cross work of Jesus Christ for the forgiveness of sins is required for initial salvation. To believe Him, specifically what He has promised in His word, is how the Christian life is lived. Because of the many false teachings regarding faith, it is important to be clear about what it means to believe, or in other words, to have faith. Armed with a correct understanding of faith itself, the spiritual man can begin to access the spiritual blessings which are his, studying God's word and cultivating a mindset of agreement with God. The mindset of faith includes trusting God, taking His viewpoint, renewing the mind with applicable truths, and keeping life's difficulties in perspective.

One of the concepts which is most basic to understanding faith is the fact that faith is not a work. To exercise biblical faith is to recognize and rest in the work of another. The scripture contrasts faith with works, showing them to be opposites:

> *But to him that worketh not, but believeth on him that justifieth the ungodly, his faith is counted for righteousness.* (Ro 4:5)

The Bible defines faith as being persuaded that something is true or right; it is to be convinced:

> *Even as Abraham believed God, and it was accounted to him for righteousness.* (Gal 3:6)

> *For what saith the scripture? Abraham believed God, and it was counted unto him for righteousness.* (Ro 4:3)

*He staggered not at the promise of God through
unbelief; but was strong in faith, giving glory
to God; And being fully persuaded that, what
he had promised, he was able also to perform.*
(Ro 4:20-21)

*One man esteemeth one day above another:
another esteemeth every day* alike. *Let every
man be fully persuaded in his own mind.*
(Ro 14:5)

To have saving faith is to be convinced that Jesus
Christ is who He says He is, and that His sacrifice on
the cross did indeed accomplish what he claimed. To
believe thusly is to trust Him for salvation. Faith for
Christian living is to believe that God can and will
accomplish what He promises to do in every saint
who is willing to cooperate with Him. Willingness
is a result of aligning one's viewpoint with God's and
agreeing that God's way is best.

The Renewing of the Mind

> *That ye be not soon shaken in mind, or be troubled...* (2 Th 2:2a)

A spiritual man operates by the power of God's grace, accessed by faith in His promises. A mindset of faith is not man's natural way of thinking. His enemies—the world, the flesh and the devil—continually bombard his mind with distractions, temptations and lies. In order to rest in the peace and comfort promised to the church, the believer must adjust his mindset to align with God's viewpoint. This is accomplished as he renews his mind at each opportunity with the truth of God's word.

> *And be not conformed to this world: but be ye transformed by the renewing of your mind, that ye may prove what is that good, and acceptable, and perfect, will of God.* (Ro 12:2)

*...but though our outward man perish, yet
the inward* man *is renewed day by day.*
(2 Cor 4:16b)

And be renewed in the spirit of your mind;
(Eph 4:23)

Let us therefore, as many as be perfect
(mature), *be thus minded: and if in any thing
ye be otherwise minded, God shall reveal even
this unto you.* (Phl 3:15, synonym added)

To enjoy the benefits of faith, the believer must
actively protect his mind. If he does not allow it to
wander, he will not be shaken by circumstances,
people, or "what-if's," but will be stabilized by his
knowledge of God's sufficiency and faithfulness.

*If ye then be risen with Christ, seek those things
which are above, where Christ sitteth on the
right hand of God. Set your affection on* (mind,
i.e. frame your thinking and reflect upon)
things above, not on things on the earth. For

21

ye are dead, and your life is hid with Christ in God. When Christ, who is our life, shall appear, then shall ye also appear with him in glory. (Col 3:1-4, clarification added)

Finally, brethren, whatsoever things are true, whatsoever things are honest, whatsoever things are just, whatsoever things are pure, whatsoever things are lovely, whatsoever things are of good report; if there be any virtue, and if there be any praise, think on these things. Those things, which ye have both learned, and received, and heard, and seen in me, do: and the God of peace shall be with you. ... Not that I speak in respect of want: for I have learned, in whatsoever state I am, therewith to be content. I know both how to be abased, and I know how to abound: every where and in all things I am instructed both to be full and to be hungry, both to abound and to suffer need. I can do all things through Christ which strengtheneth me. (Phl 4:8-9, 11-13)

But let it be *the hidden man of the heart, in that which is not corruptible,* even the ornament *of a meek and quiet* (tranquil, unruffled, undisturbed) *spirit, which is in the sight of God of great price.* (1 Pet 3:4, synonyms added)

For God hath not given us the spirit of fear; but of power, and of love, and of a sound mind. (2 Tim 1:7)

There is no fear in love; but perfect love casteth out fear: because fear hath torment. (1 Jhn 4:18a)

The letters to the church instruct the believer on how to bear spiritual fruit such as peace, contentment and self-control. The Old Testament is equally important as it is filled with descriptions of God's character, and narratives of His works. The history of God's dealings with Israel and others teach the Christian that he can confidently place his hope in God; his conviction and confident expectation is that God is always good and that He always keeps His promises.

> *For whatsoever things were written aforetime were written for our learning, that we through patience and comfort of the scriptures might have hope. ... Now the God of hope fill you with all joy and peace in believing, that ye may abound in hope, through the power of the Holy Ghost.* (Ro 15:4, 13)

The enemies of the believer wish to frighten and intimate him. If he cannot be frightened, he might be tempted. If he cannot be tempted, he can be kept busy—too busy to know the scriptures well enough that he can use them for daily living. He does not know or perhaps has forgotten that God will honor every moment that he devotes to God's word. If the believer succumbs to the enemies' attacks, he can recover by renewing his mind with applicable scriptures. One of the first things he might do is to remind himself that the troubles of this world will soon pass away.

Holding a Correct Perspective

Be ye also patient; stablish (stabilize) *your hearts: for the coming of the Lord draweth nigh.* (Jas 5:8, synonym added)

In difficult times, a Christian can begin to take on the viewpoint of the world. Disgusted by what he sees around him, he can be overtaken by feelings of hopelessness, discouragement and exhaustion. Fear or anxiety about events in his life might paralyze him, keeping him from appropriating the power and victory which is his. Holding in mind the perspective of God is vital for him to continue to live by faith.

Because a Christian's hope is not in this world, he is able, by faith, to view the world and its troubles as they really are: temporary, fleeting, and in many ways small when compared to the glory that awaits him in the world to come. This perspective allows him to rise above his circumstances, not losing sight of the work he has to do—to share the Gospel with the lost, to minister to the saints, and to live a God-honoring life that gives credibility to his testimony of Jesus Christ. To remain Spirit-filled, he returns again and again to the scriptures to counteract the worldly messages with which he is bombarded. The truth of God's word renews his mind, enabling him to maintain a proper perspective of life's difficulties and to display God's work within him.

> *For I reckon that the sufferings of this present time* are *not worthy to be compared with the glory which shall be revealed in us.* (Ro 8:18)

> We are *troubled on every side, yet not distressed;* we are *perplexed, but not in despair; Persecuted, but not forsaken; cast down, but not destroyed; Always bearing about in the body the dying of the Lord Jesus, that the life also of Jesus might be made manifest in our body. For we which live are alway delivered unto death for Jesus' sake,* **that the life also of Jesus might be made manifest in our mortal flesh**. *So then death worketh in us, but life in you. We having the same spirit of*

faith, according as it is written, I believed, and therefore have I spoken; we also believe, and therefore speak; Knowing that he which raised up the Lord Jesus shall raise up us also by Jesus, and shall present us with you. For all things are for your sakes, that the abundant grace might through the thanksgiving of many redound to the glory of God. For which cause we faint not; but though our outward man perish, yet the inward man is renewed day by day. For our light affliction, which is but for a moment, worketh for us a far more exceeding and eternal weight of glory; While we look not at the things which are seen, but at the things which are not seen: for the things which are seen are temporal; but the things which are not seen are eternal. (2 Cor 4:8-18)

God is trying to accomplish something in every believer—to conform him to the image of Christ, thereby preparing him for life in His presence. God understands that life is difficult and that it includes many painful hardships. The eternal perspective that

He is trying to teach His children includes having correct expectations. Believing that things should always go well is not only unrealistic in a fallen world, it is a set-up for disappointment and extreme, unhelpful reactions. For American Christians, most things go extraordinarily well when compared to the lives of Christians in history and in much of the rest of the world. Nonetheless, suffering should be expected, not with morbid dread, but with confidence in God's sufficient provision. Christ's suffering on earth prepared Him to be a perfect high priest who understands everything that His brethren endure.

> *For it became him, for whom* are *all things, and by whom* are *all things, in bringing many sons unto glory, to make the captain of their salvation perfect through sufferings.* (Heb 2:10)

> *For in that He Himself has suffered, being tempted, He is able to aid those who are tempted.* (Heb 2:18 NKJV)

Seeing then that we have a great high priest, that is passed into the heavens, Jesus the Son of God, let us hold fast our *profession. For we have not an high priest which cannot be touched with the feeling of our infirmities; but was in all points tempted like as* we are, yet *without sin. Let us therefore come boldly unto the throne of grace, that we may obtain mercy, and find grace to help in time of need.* (Heb 4:14-16)

Though he were a Son, yet learned he obedience by the things which he suffered; And being made perfect, he became the author of eternal salvation unto all them that obey him; (Heb 5:8-9)

For unto you it is given in the behalf of Christ, not only to believe on him, but also to suffer for his sake... (Phl 1:29)

By whom also we have access by faith into this grace wherein we stand, and rejoice in hope of the glory of God. And not only so, but we glory in tribulations also: knowing that tribulation worketh patience; And patience, experience; and experience, hope: And hope maketh not ashamed; because the love of God is shed abroad in our hearts by the Holy Ghost which is given unto us. (Ro 5:2-5)

And we know that all things work together for good to them that love God, to them who are the called according to his purpose. (Ro 8:28, lit. "are loving God," i.e. they are spiritual)

And sent Timotheus, our brother, and minister of God, and our fellowlabourer in the gospel of Christ, to establish you, and to comfort you concerning your faith: That no man should be moved by these afflictions: for yourselves know that we are appointed thereunto. For verily, when we were with you, we told you before that we should suffer tribulation; even as it came to pass, and ye know. For this cause, when I could no longer forbear, I sent to know your faith, lest by some means the tempter have tempted you, and our labour be in vain. But now when Timotheus came from you unto us, and brought us good tidings of your faith and charity, and that ye have good remembrance of us always, desiring greatly to see us, as we also to see you: Therefore, brethren, we were comforted over you in all our affliction and distress by your faith: For now we live, if ye stand fast in the Lord. For what thanks can we render to God again for you, for all the joy wherewith we joy for your sakes before our God; Night and day praying exceedingly that we might see your face, and might perfect that which is lacking in your faith? Now God himself and our Father, and our Lord Jesus Christ, direct our way unto you. And the Lord make you to increase and abound in love one toward another, and toward all men, even as we do toward you: To the end he may

*stablish your hearts unblameable in holiness
before God, even our Father, at the coming
of our Lord Jesus Christ with all his saints.*
(1 Th 3:2-13)

*Wherein ye greatly rejoice, though now for a
season, if need be, ye are in heaviness through
manifold temptations: That the trial of your
faith, being much more precious than of gold
that perisheth, though it be tried with fire,
might be found unto praise and honour and
glory at the appearing of Jesus Christ: ...
Wherefore gird up the loins of your mind, be
sober, and hope to the end for the grace that
is to be brought unto you at the revelation
of Jesus Christ; As obedient children, not
fashioning yourselves according to the former
lusts in your ignorance: But as he which hath
called you is holy, so be ye holy in all manner of
conversation; Because it is written, Be ye holy;
for I am holy.* (1 Pet 1:6-7, 13-16)

Because the believer has a high priest to whom he can go for well-timed help, and because he is able to hold a proper perspective of the trials in life, he can confidently turn to the scriptures for all that he needs to endure. The Christian life is a faith-rest life. It begins with faith in a person and continues by faith in the promises of God. By knowing and believing what God has promised to the church, and taking the time to allow the Spirit to bring it to mind for its use, every functional Christian can experience the joy, peace, self-control, patience, and love that was displayed by Jesus Christ Himself. He can rest in God's sufficiency without anxiety, fear, frustration, or despair. Using the truth of God's word to operate by the power of His grace does in every case enable the Christian to live in blessing and victory, even in the most difficult circumstances.

And the Word was made flesh, and dwelt among us, (and we beheld his glory, the glory as of the only begotten of the Father,) full of grace and truth. (Jhn 1:14)

For the law was given by Moses, but grace and truth came by Jesus Christ. (Jhn 1:17)

Which is come unto you, as it is in all the world; and bringeth forth fruit, as it doth also in you, since the day ye heard of it, and knew the grace of God in truth: (Col 1:6)

Chapter 3

Faith: How it Works

We then, as *workers together* with him,
beseech you *also that ye receive not the*
grace of God in vain. (2 Cor 6:1)

The life of faith begins with the conviction that God
will do what He has promised in his letters to the
church. Those who believe Him are able to view the
world as He does, holding an eternal perspective and
using grace doctrine for the renewing of the mind.
To exercise faith in the promises of God is to say,
"Yes," to God, allowing Him to fill the believer with
spiritual understanding, wisdom and power. In this
Spirit-filled condition, the Christian can access the
blessings of living by faith.

The Christian life is a faith-rest life. This means that
by faith the spiritual man rests in God's provision
for him, just as he did for initial salvation. In both

cases he is relying upon God; only the object of his faith has changed slightly, from Christ's payment for sins, to the promise of power for living through His resurrection.

> *There remaineth therefore a rest to the people of God. For he that is entered into his rest, he also hath ceased from his own works, as God did from his. Let us labour therefore to enter into that rest, lest any man fall after the same example of unbelief.* (Heb 4:9-11)

> *As ye have therefore received Christ Jesus the Lord* (i.e. by faith), so *walk ye in him: Rooted and built up in him, and stablished in the faith, as ye have been taught, abounding therein with thanksgiving.* (Col 2:6-7, clarification added)

To live by faith is not to delve into one's own personal determination to try harder and do more. Faith is instead the conviction that God will do as He promised. It includes a mindset of dependence upon God, even in those things which one is able to do without any help. This is so because the life of faith is not an emergency back-up but rather it is a quality of life that is produced only by God Himself. The spiritual man must know and understand what God has promised and trust in it, to the exclusion of all else.

Every Christian is either exercising faith and is a spiritual man, or he is operating independently from God, and he is a carnal (fleshly) man. It is not possible for a Christian to be partly spiritual and partly carnal, trusting God to a certain degree, but hedging his bets on some other remedy. Independence from God to any degree is sin, even if the act is not manifestly evil. Nothing produced apart from God is acceptable to Him, because the source of those things is one's sinful human nature.

So then they that are (operating) *in the flesh cannot please God.* (Ro 8:8, clarification added; Paul coined the usage of the word "flesh" to refer to the body indwelt by the law of sin, aka principle of sin, often called the sin nature)

And he that doubteth is damned if he eat,
because he eateth not of faith: for whatsoever is
not of faith is sin. (Ro 4:23)

But without faith it is impossible to please
him… (Heb 11:6a)

The believer who is resting in God's sufficiency trusts and depends upon God to provide for him; God's response to his faith is to produce within him whatever he needs, whether it be wisdom, courage, calm, faithfulness, determination, or other similar spiritual virtues. These, in turn, enable him to make right choices and to do what is needed because God even provides the ability.

I am crucified with Christ: nevertheless I live;
*yet not I, but **Christ liveth in me**: and the life*
which I now live in the flesh I live by the faith of
the Son of God, who loved me, and gave himself
for me. (Gal 2:20)

*For it is God which **worketh in you** both to will*
and to do of his good pleasure. (Phl 2:13)

*Whereunto I also labour, striving according to his working, which **worketh in me** mightily.* (Col 1:29)

*That he would grant you, according to the riches of his glory, to be strengthened with might by his Spirit **in the inner man**; That Christ may dwell in your hearts by faith; that ye, being rooted and grounded in love, …
And to know the love of Christ, which passeth knowledge, that ye might be **filled with all the fulness of God**. Now unto him that is able to do exceeding abundantly above all that we ask or think, according to the power that **worketh in us**,* (Eph 3:16-17, 19-20)

*For this cause also thank we God without ceasing, because, when ye received the word of God which ye heard of us, ye received it not as the word of men, but as it is in truth, the word of God, **which effectually worketh also in you that believe**.* (1 Th 2:13)

Blessed be *the God and Father of our Lord Jesus Christ, who hath blessed us with **all** spiritual blessings in heavenly* places *in Christ:* (Eph 1:3)

A Christian's faith in God's promises make those promises actual in his experience. Through faith, he is laying hold on an eternal quality of life for use in his earthly life. In a small way he is a partaker in the divine nature, enjoying the benefits of the grace of God.

*Whereby are given unto us exceeding great and precious promises: **that by these** ye might be partakers of the divine nature, having escaped the corruption that is in the world through lust.* (2 Pet 1:4)

Fight the good fight of faith, lay hold on eternal life, whereunto thou art also called, and hast professed a good profession before many witnesses. (1 Tim 6:12)

Laying up in store for themselves a good foundation against the time to come, that they may lay hold on eternal life. (1 Tim 6:19)

The enemies of the Christian work to enslave him, using fleshly cravings, worldly distractions, and demonic philosophies, often delivered through emotional (soulish) ploys. The body of grace doctrine sets him free by revealing and contradicting these traps. A Christian who is Spirit-filled through faith in God's promises is able to recognize these errors; He aligns himself with God and lives instead in the power of spiritual victory.

And ye shall know the truth, and the truth shall make you free. (Jhn 8:32)

For though we walk in the flesh, we do not war after the flesh: (For the weapons of our warfare are not carnal, but mighty through God to the pulling down of strong holds;) Casting down imaginations, and every high thing that

> *exalteth itself against the knowledge of God,
> and bringing into captivity every thought to the
> obedience of Christ;* (2 Cor 10:3-5)

> *This I say then, Walk in the Spirit, and ye shall
> not fulfil the lust of the flesh.* (Gal 5:16)

Directing Faith Toward the Promises of God

> *But we have the mind of Christ.* (1 Cor 2:16b)

> *Let this mind be in you, which was also in
> Christ Jesus…* (Phl 2:5)

Every person who is born again is indwelt by God
and has the mind of Christ. Therefore, he can
view and experience each situation with the same
response to it that God has. His conviction and
assurance of God's sufficiency leads him to look to
the scriptures and believe. God's word instructs him
so that when he faces difficult times, he knows that
he will come out on the other side of the trial with
increased wisdom, endurance, and trust in God.

Living by faith has as many facets as there are experiences in life. Faith can be applied to all aspects of living, no matter how unusual or mundane, because God is not surprised by any of life's occurrences. The Christian can be assured that God has already provided him with the ability to cope graciously with them all, and to do whatever is needed in the situation. God knows everything that His children will face in life. He does not leave His children alone or helpless. Through the simple action of directing faith toward the promises to the church, the spiritual man is fully equipped for every situation that he encounters, whether or not he has experienced something similar before.

> *All scripture* is *given by inspiration of God, and* is *profitable for doctrine, for reproof, for correction, for instruction in righteousness: That the man of God may be perfect,* **throughly furnished** *unto all good works.*
> (2 Tim 3:16-17)

> *Grace and peace be multiplied unto you*
> *through the knowledge of God, and of Jesus*
> *our Lord, According as his divine power hath*
> *given unto us **all things** that pertain unto*
> *life and godliness, through the knowledge of*
> *him that hath called us to glory and virtue*
> (2 Pet 1:2-3)

> *And God is able to make **all grace** abound*
> *toward you; that ye, always **having all***
> ***sufficiency in all** things, may abound to every*
> *good work…* (2 Cor 9:8)

Whether or not a Christian has the needed characteristics naturally has no bearing whatsoever. God has them and God indwells him. These qualities are accessed by faith; they become actual in the saint because he believes what God has said. His faith allows God to fill him with divine enablement, thinking and responding in ways he never did before. Even his natural attributes are taken to another level. The believer does not grit his teeth and try with all his might to produce the right attitude or reaction. He does not "develop" them by hard work, perseverance, or practice. He knows that they are already his and he believes it. He faces a stressor and says to himself, "I know God has enabled me to react to this correctly. I believe Him." He takes a moment to consider an applicable scripture and responds with supernatural fortitude. As he matures, he begins to apply spirituality to more areas of his life, realizing that God empowers him to do everything with joy and gratitude. Even in tragedy, the spiritual man is able to maintain his Spirit-filled condition. He is rightfully saddened, angry or disappointed, but he quickly adjusts himself, directing his faith toward God's provision. He does not dwell on his circumstances or those who contributed to them. He knows that suffering and loss is a normal part of life in this fallen world, so he is not thrown off course when things do not go his way.

For unto you it is given in the behalf of Christ, not only to believe on him, but also to suffer for his sake; (Phl 1:29)

For this is thankworthy, if a man for conscience
toward God endure grief, suffering wrongfully.
For what glory is it, if, when ye be buffeted
for your faults, ye shall take it patiently?
but if, when ye do well, and suffer for it, ye
take it patiently, this is acceptable with God.
(1 Pet 2:19-20)

Wherefore let them that suffer according to the
will of God commit the keeping of their souls to
him in well doing, as unto a faithful Creator.
(1 Pet 4:19)

But the God of all grace, who hath called us
unto his eternal glory by Christ Jesus, after
that ye have suffered a while, make you perfect,
stablish, strengthen, settle you. (1 Pet 5:10)

Nobody enjoys the difficult times of life. They can stumble any believer, no matter how long he has been saved. The great high priest, Jesus Christ, was tempted, tested, and suffered for the sake of all those who will believe. Because of the fall of mankind into sin, this world is cursed with sin. God understands the suffering that every person endures, and desires that everlasting good would come from it. To that end, He provided a platinum package of spiritual benefits, available to every saint the very instant he believes the Gospel of Christ and is regenerated. By knowing and believing what God says about him, the Christian can enjoy the riches of God's grace, experiencing the great love of God and the plethora of spiritual blessings that He has showered upon his children. The supernatural outworking of the virtues of the Savior completely changes the quality of the Christian's life. His attitude, reactions, and choices are a blessing, a help, and a testimony to others, bringing God the glory He deserves.

Chapter 4

Faith: How it Looks

That ye would walk worthy of God, who hath called
you unto his kingdom and glory. (1 Th 2:12)

The Christian walk of faith begins with the
conviction that God will always act in accordance
with His character and word. It continues with the
knowledge of the promises contained in His word,
which are made actual by faith. In order to walk
by faith consistently, the Christian must learn how
to recognize the outworking of those promises in
himself. He must know the difference between God's
character and the traits of his own sinful nature so
that he can return to operating by faith when he
departs from it.

As a Christian learns the doctrines of grace, they may
seem like an enormous to-do list of works. The call
to study, to pray, to worship, to evangelize the lost,

to serve the brethren through hospitality, giving, assembling, helping, teaching, encouraging, and so much more can seem like an insurmountable project list. But the Christian life is not one of religious works; it is a spiritual relationship characterized primarily by love. Godly character and good works are the natural result of living by faith. The person who is filled with God's fullness sees good things to do everywhere he looks. He does not have to invent things to do, create projects, or pressure others to do more. The spiritual man bears spiritual fruit because he believes God. By emanating the character of God in all that he does, his activities count as good works, because their source is God Himself.

> *As we have therefore opportunity, let us do good unto all* men, *especially unto them who are of the household of faith.* (Gal 6:10)

Often it is the difficult times in life which drive Christians to delve deeply into the meaning and operation of faith. The pressure of life reveals the need to depend completely upon God. In this way, even a short-term trial can bring about a good outcome with a long-term benefit. If the Christian applies what he learned to his everyday life, he will learn to walk by faith consistently; to do so is to spiritually mature.

In some cases, a believer will live by faith through the trial, but then return to depending upon himself after it ends. This is why some look back at the hard times in life as some of the best times. What they might not realize is that what made the hard times so satisfying was that they were empowered by grace and were experiencing supernatural peace, confidence, contentment, or comfort, among many other possibilities. The Christian who can recognize spiritual fruit in himself can learn to produce it at will. The moment he recognizes the lack of these spiritual blessings, he can return to the condition of spirituality by faith. When he takes opportunities in his daily routine to set his mind upon the truth, the doctrines of grace act like a mirror. If he sees God's character in himself, he knows he is a spiritual man. If he does not, he knows he is a carnal man, and he can renew his mind with the truth, returning to agreement with God. The truth of God's word counteracts his natural bend toward fleshly and soulish products such as impatience, cowardice, laziness, ill-temperedness, lack of self-control, fear, anxiety, discouragement, and emotion-driven responses. The mirror of grace teaches the Christian so that he is able to recognize his spiritual condition. Many verses describe what spirituality looks like.

> *But the fruit of the Spirit is love, joy, peace, longsuffering, gentleness, goodness, faith, Meekness, temperance…* (Gal 5:22-23a)

> Let *love be without dissimulation. Abhor that which is evil; cleave to that which is good.* Be *kindly affectioned one to another with brotherly love; in honour preferring one another; Not slothful in business; fervent in spirit; serving the Lord; Rejoicing in hope; patient in tribulation; continuing instant in prayer; Distributing to the necessity of saints; given to hospitality.* (Ro 12:9-13)

Wherein he hath abounded toward us in all wisdom and prudence; (Eph 1:8)

I therefore, the prisoner of the Lord, beseech you that ye walk worthy of the vocation wherewith ye are called, With all lowliness and meekness, with longsuffering, forbearing one another in love; Endeavouring to keep the unity of the Spirit in the bond of peace. (Eph 4:1-3)

Let no corrupt communication proceed out of your mouth, but that which is good to the use of edifying, that it may minister grace unto the hearers. And grieve not the holy Spirit of God, whereby ye are sealed unto the day of redemption. Let all bitterness, and wrath, and anger, and clamour, and evil speaking, be put away from you, with all malice: And be ye kind one to another, tenderhearted, forgiving one another, even as God for Christ's sake hath forgiven you. (Eph 4:29-32)

Do all things without murmurings and disputings: That ye may be blameless and harmless, the sons of God, without rebuke, in the midst of a crooked and perverse nation, among whom ye shine as lights in the world; Holding forth the word of life; that I may rejoice in the day of Christ, that I have not run in vain, neither laboured in vain. (Phl 2:14-16)

For this cause we also, since the day we heard it, do not cease to pray for you, and to desire that ye might be filled with the knowledge of his will in all wisdom and spiritual understanding; That ye might walk worthy of the Lord unto all pleasing, being fruitful in every good work, and increasing in the knowledge of God; Strengthened with all might, according to his glorious power, unto all patience and longsuffering with joyfulness; (Col 1:9-11)

That their hearts might be comforted, being knit together in love, and unto all riches of the full assurance of understanding, to the

acknowledgement of the mystery of God, and of the Father, and of Christ... For though I be absent in the flesh, yet am I with you in the spirit, joying and beholding your order, and the stedfastness of your faith in Christ. (Col 2:2, 5)

But ye are a chosen generation, a royal priesthood, an holy nation, a peculiar people; that ye should shew forth the praises of him who hath called you out of darkness into his marvellous light: (1 Pet 2:9)

Use hospitality one to another without grudging. (1 Pet 4:9)

Moreover, brethren, we do you to wit of the grace of God bestowed on the churches of Macedonia; How that in a great trial of affliction the abundance of their joy and their deep poverty abounded unto the riches of their liberality. For to their power, I bear record, yea, and beyond their power they were willing of themselves; Praying us with much intreaty that we would receive the gift, and take upon us *the fellowship of the ministering to the saints. And* this they did, *not as we hoped, but first gave their own selves to the Lord, and unto us by the will of God.* (2 Cor 8:1-5)

Now therefore perform the doing of it; *that as* there was *a readiness to will, so* there may be *a performance also out of that which ye have. For if there be first a willing mind, it is accepted according to that a man hath,* and *not according to that he hath not. For* I mean *not that other men be eased, and ye burdened: But by an equality,* that *now at this time your abundance* may be a supply *for their want, that their abundance also may be* a supply *for your want: that there may be equality: As it is written, He that* had gathered *much* had *nothing over; and he that* had gathered *little had no lack.* (2 Cor 8:11-15)

It should be obvious from these verses that these qualities and acts of service are expectations for every functional Christian. The word of God is complete. It lacks nothing, and its sufficiency facilitates the same in the saints that they might minister to the body of Christ according to its needs, as well as minster the Gospel to the lost. For example, the spiritual man makes a passing comment to a stranger, mentioning God, the Bible, church, or something similar. If a discussion ensues, he shares the Gospel of Christ, 1 Corinthians 15:1-4. If he knows that another Christian has a need, he meets that need if he is able. He is generous in giving to those ministries which adhere to the will of God because he is eager to see others saved, and the body of Christ supported. Natural abilities can be of help, but are not necessary. Faith in God's promises supplies any lacking in desire or ability, filling up the believer with everything necessary to cope with troubles, minister to others, and enjoy an elevated quality of life.

> *That the communication of thy faith may become effectual by the acknowledging of every good thing which is in you in Christ Jesus.* (Phm 1:6)

God's word is filled with descriptions of difficult times and what the spiritual man's response to them is to be. This does not mean that the saint must figure out how to behave in this way. It is to teach him what to look for in himself, and what to believe if he does not see it. For example, in regard to anxiety and worry he must believe the teaching that he is to be anxious for nothing but instead be at peace.

> *Humble yourselves therefore under the mighty hand of God, that he may exalt you in due time: Casting all your care upon him; for he careth for you.* (1 Pet 5:6-7)

> *Let your moderation be known unto all men. The Lord is at hand. Be careful* (anxious) *for nothing; but in every thing by prayer and supplication with thanksgiving let your requests be made known unto God. And the peace of God, which passeth all understanding, shall keep your hearts and minds through Christ Jesus.* (Phl 4:5-7, synonym added)

And let the peace of God rule in your hearts, to the which also ye are called in one body; and be ye thankful. (Col 3:15)

God gave His written word, and he also sent a person to comfort and help His children. When Jesus' earthly ministry ended, God sent the Holy Spirit who supplies abundant comfort both supernaturally and through the ministry of the body of Christ. This comfort is available by faith.

And I will pray the Father, and he shall give you another Comforter, that he may abide with you for ever... (Jhn 14:16)

That is, that I may be comforted together with you by the mutual faith both of you and me. (Ro 1:12)

Blessed be God, even the Father of our Lord Jesus Christ, the Father of mercies, and the God of all comfort; Who comforteth us in all our tribulation, that we may be able to comfort

*them which are in any trouble, by the comfort
wherewith we ourselves are comforted of God.*
(2 Cor 1:3-4)

*Great is my boldness of speech toward you,
great is my glorying of you: I am filled with
comfort, I am exceeding joyful in all our
tribulation.* (2 Cor 7:4)

*Now our Lord Jesus Christ himself, and God,
even our Father, which hath loved us, and
hath given us everlasting consolation and good
hope through grace, Comfort your hearts, and
stablish you in every good word and work.*
(2 Th 2:16-17)

Many things in life are not as one would wish them
to be. God enables the spiritual man to be content
in his circumstances so that his ministry is not
hindered by the temptation to become occupied
with earthly desires for gain:

Not that I speak in respect of want: for I have learned, in whatsoever state I am, therewith *to be content...* (Phl 4:11)

But godliness with contentment is great gain. For we brought nothing into this *world,* and it is *certain we can carry nothing out. And having food and raiment let us be therewith content. ... But thou, O man of God, flee these things; and follow after righteousness, godliness, faith, love, patience, meekness.* (1 Tim 6:6-8, 11)

Life's difficulties can make even a mature believer feel weak. He must be spiritual in order to overcome feelings of hopelessness or despair. The spiritual man is strong because he depends upon the Lord for his strength:

Finally, my brethren, be strong in the Lord, and in the power of his might. (Eph 6:10)

> *Thou therefore, my son, be strong in the grace that is in Christ Jesus.* (2 Tim 2:1)

By faith, he can endure hardship:

> *Thou therefore endure hardness, as a good soldier of Jesus Christ.* (2 Tim 2:3)

As the spiritual man experiences victorious living, he is motivated to learn more. God wants him to learn and enables him to understand, remember, and implement grace doctrine, the "how-to" teachings for Christian living. The Holy Spirit brings to mind the truths that he needs; the more doctrine that he knows, the more the Spirit has to use so that He might help him.

> *Consider what I say; and the Lord give thee understanding in all things.* (2 Tim 2:7)

> *Wherefore be ye not unwise, but understanding what the will of the Lord is.* (Eph 5:17)

For this cause we also, since the day we heard it, do not cease to pray for you, and to desire that ye might be filled with the knowledge of his will in all wisdom and spiritual understanding... (Col 1:9)

Howbeit when he, the Spirit of truth, is come, he will guide you into all truth... (Jhn 16:13a)

Wherefore I will not be negligent to put you always in remembrance of these things, though ye know them, *and be established **in the present truth**.* (2 Pet 1:12, emphasis added)

But the Comforter, which is *the Holy Ghost, whom the Father will send in my name, he shall teach you all things, and bring all things to your remembrance, whatsoever I have said unto you.* (Jhn 14:26)

The usefulness of spirituality is without limit. Regardless of how trying the situation, every Christian can have endless patience—because God does:

*But in all things approving ourselves as
the ministers of God, in much patience, in
afflictions, in necessities, in distresses ...*
(2 Cor 6:4)

*Strengthened with all might, according to
his glorious power, unto all patience and
longsuffering with joyfulness... (Col 1:11)*

*Now we exhort you, brethren, warn them
that are unruly, comfort the feebleminded,
support the weak, be patient toward all men.*
(1 Th 5:14)

*So that we ourselves glory in you in the
churches of God for your patience and faith in
all your persecutions and tribulations that ye
endure... (2 Th 1:4)*

Many trials in life include an element of temptation.
The temptation might be to return to operating as
one did before regeneration. It might be to lash
out, to give up, to blame God, or do things which

would harm one's testimony, one's life, or the life of someone else. The spiritual man is able to both resist temptation and mature by doing so. He looks to grace doctrine with faith which produces spiritual fruit to the glory of God:

The Lord knoweth how to deliver the godly out of temptations, and to reserve the unjust unto the day of judgment to be punished: (2 Pet 2:9)

My brethren, count it all joy when ye fall into divers temptations; Knowing this, *that the trying of your faith worketh patience. But let patience have* her *perfect work, that ye may be perfect and entire* (mature and complete), *wanting* (lacking) *nothing.* (Jas 1:2-4, synonyms added)

Flee also youthful lusts: but follow righteousness, faith, charity, peace, with them that call on the Lord out of a pure heart. But foolish and unlearned questions avoid, knowing that they do gender strifes. And the

> *servant of the Lord must not strive; but be*
> *gentle unto all men, apt to teach, patient…*
> (2 Tim 2:22-24)

> *Dearly beloved, I beseech you as strangers and*
> *pilgrims, abstain from fleshly lusts, which war*
> *against the soul …* (1 Pet 2:11)

If he fails to resist temptation, he knows that he is carnal. To return to spirituality he must renew his mind with truth and ask himself if he truly believes and desires it. The priorities and goals of the spiritual man are the same as God's. He recognizes and appreciates their eternal value, and he has determined that he will continue in them.

> *But what things were gain to me, those I*
> *counted loss for Christ. Yea doubtless, and I*
> *count all things but loss for the excellency of*
> *the knowledge of Christ Jesus my Lord: for*
> *whom I have suffered the loss of all things,*
> *and do count them but dung, that I may win*
> *Christ, And be found in him, not having*

mine own righteousness, which is of the law, but that which is through the faith of Christ, the righteousness which is of God by faith: That I may know him, and the power of his resurrection, and the fellowship of his sufferings, being made conformable unto his death; ... Brethren, I count not myself to have apprehended: but this *one thing* I do, *forgetting those things which are behind, and reaching forth unto those things which are before, I press toward the mark for the prize of the high calling of God in Christ Jesus.* (Phl 3:7-10, 13-14)

Wherefore seeing we also are compassed about with so great a cloud of witnesses, let us lay aside every weight, and the sin which doth so easily beset us, *and let us run with patience the race that is set before us, Looking unto Jesus the author and finisher of* our *faith; who for the joy that was set before him endured the cross, despising the shame, and is set down at the right hand of the throne of God. For consider him that endured such contradiction of sinners against himself, lest ye be wearied and faint in your minds. Ye have not yet resisted unto blood, striving against sin.* (Heb 12:1-4)

Some turn to faith in the worst of times, but God intends for it to help the saints every day. There are difficult things that Christians encounter routinely; such things are so ordinary that it does not occur to them that operating by faith is applicable. For example, laws are not always just nor justly enforced. Employers can be demanding and unfair. Family members are loved, and yet they can also be trying at times. The spiritual man does not focus on the injustices of this world. His hope is in the perfect justice to come. He cooperates with the rules at home, obeys the laws of the land, and submits to authority. He cooperates with teachers at school or supervisors at work and is well-spoken. He is a benefit to them because he looks to God's word to empower him to do so:

Obey them that have the rule over you, and submit yourselves: for they watch for your souls, as they that must give account, that they may do it with joy, and not with grief: for that is unprofitable for you. (Heb 13:17)

Submit yourselves to every ordinance of man for the Lord's sake: whether it be to the king, as supreme... (1 Pet 2:13)

In a heated situation, he takes a moment to let the Holy Spirit minister to him. He is then able to control his temper and his tongue:

Wherefore, my beloved brethren, let every man be swift to hear, slow to speak, slow to wrath: (Jas 1:19)

The Christian who operates in knowledge and faith recognizes that the trials of life on earth will not end until Christ's return. He adjusts his expectations accordingly and reminds himself that he does not know it all. When he recognizes carnality in himself, he returns to God's word for correction. His teachable attitude makes him credible, compassionate, merciful and much more.

> *But the wisdom that is from above is first pure, then peaceable, gentle, and easy to be intreated, full of mercy and good fruits, without partiality, and without hypocrisy.* (Jas 3:17)

> *Likewise, ye husbands, dwell with them according to knowledge, giving honour unto the wife, as unto the weaker vessel, and as being heirs together of the grace of life; that your prayers be not hindered. Finally, be ye all of one mind, having compassion one of another, love as brethren, be pitiful, be courteous: Not rendering evil for evil, or railing for railing: but contrariwise blessing; knowing that ye are thereunto called, that ye should inherit a blessing.* (1 Pet 3:7-9)

The faith-rest life is founded on knowing God's written word and trusting in Him. Faith is the Christian's conviction that God keeps His promises, and that those promises will completely equip him for whatever he must face. The believer who rests in the sufficiency of grace through faith can weather any storm in life, emerging with a testimony of the love and power of God—not because he worked really hard or tried to be good, but because he knows the God who is always good.

> *That ye may with one mind* and *one mouth glorify God, even the Father of our Lord Jesus Christ.* (Ro 15:6)

Conclusion

God's Provision is Sufficient

Not that we are sufficient of ourselves to think any thing as of ourselves; but our sufficiency is of God; (2 Cor 3:5)

Please be encouraged by the many verses that provide assurance of God's faithfulness and provision! Believe and rejoice!

Nay, in all these things we are more than conquerors through him that loved us. (Ro 8:37)

For all the promises of God in him are yea, and in him Amen, unto the glory of God by us. (2 Cor 1:20)

Now thanks be unto God, which always causeth us to triumph in Christ, and maketh manifest the savour of his knowledge by us in every place. (2 Cor 2:14)

*But we have this treasure in earthen vessels,
that the excellency of the power may be of God,
and not of us.* (2 Cor 4:7)

*And he said unto me, My grace is sufficient
for thee: for my strength is made perfect in
weakness. Most gladly therefore will I rather
glory in my infirmities, that the power of Christ
may rest upon me.* (2 Cor 12:9)

*Being confident of this very thing, that he
which hath begun a good work in you will
perform it until the day of Jesus Christ...*
(Phl 1:6)

*And ye are complete in him, which is the head
of all principality and power...* (Col 2:10)

*If a man therefore purge himself from these, he
shall be a vessel unto honour, sanctified, and
meet for the master's use,* and *prepared unto
every good work.* (2 Tim 2:21)

Make you perfect in every good work to do his will, working in you that which is wellpleasing in his sight, through Jesus Christ; to whom be *glory for ever and ever. Amen.* (Heb 13:21)

Forasmuch as ye know that ye were not redeemed with corruptible things, as *silver and gold, from your vain conversation* received *by tradition from your fathers; But with the precious blood of Christ, as of a lamb without blemish and without spot: Who verily was foreordained before the foundation of the world, but was manifest in these last times for you, Who by him do believe in God, that raised him up from the dead, and gave him glory; that your faith and hope might be in God.* (1 Pet 1:18-21)